D1117148

SandCastle™

Giant Animals

WHALE
SHARK

ANDERS HANSON

Consulting Editor, Diane Craig, M.A./Reading Specialist

A Division of ABDO

ABDO
Publishing Company

visit us at www.abdopublishing.com

Published by ABDO Publishing Company, a division of ABDO, P.O. Box 398166, Minneapolis, Minnesota 55439. Copyright © 2014 by Abdo Consulting Group, Inc. International copyrights reserved in all countries. No part of this book may be reproduced in any form without written permission from the publisher. SandCastle™ is a trademark and logo of ABDO Publishing Company.

Printed in the United States of America, North Mankato, Minnesota
102013
012014

 PRINTED ON RECYCLED PAPER

Editor: Liz Salzmann
Content Developer: Nancy Tuminelly
Cover and Interior Design and Production: Anders Hanson, Mighty Media, Inc.
Photo Credits: Shutterstock, Thinkstock

Library of Congress Cataloging-in-Publication Data
Hanson, Anders, 1980- author.
  Whale shark / Anders Hanson ; consulting editor, Diane Craig, M.A., reading specialist.
      pages cm. -- (Giant animals)
  Audience: 4 to 9.
  ISBN 978-1-62403-062-8
1. Whale shark--Juvenile literature. I. Craig, Diane, editor. II. Title.
  QL638.95.R4H36 2014
  597.3--dc23
                          2013023930

SandCastle™ Level: Transitional

SandCastle™ books are created by a team of professional educators, reading specialists, and content developers around five essential components—phonemic awareness, phonics, vocabulary, text comprehension, and fluency—to assist young readers as they develop reading skills and strategies and increase their general knowledge. All books are written, reviewed, and leveled for guided reading, early reading intervention, and Accelerated Reader® programs for use in shared, guided, and independent reading and writing activities to support a balanced approach to literacy instruction. The SandCastle™ series has four levels that correspond to early literacy development. The levels are provided to help teachers and parents select appropriate books for young readers.

Emerging Readers
(no flags)

Beginning Readers
(1 flag)

Transitional Readers
(2 flags)

Fluent Readers
(3 flags)

contents

HELLO, WHALE SHARK!

WHALE SHARK,
40 FEET (12 M)

←

Whale sharks are the biggest fish in the ocean!
Whale sharks grow up to 40 feet (12 m) long.
They weigh up to 47,000 pounds (21,319 kg).

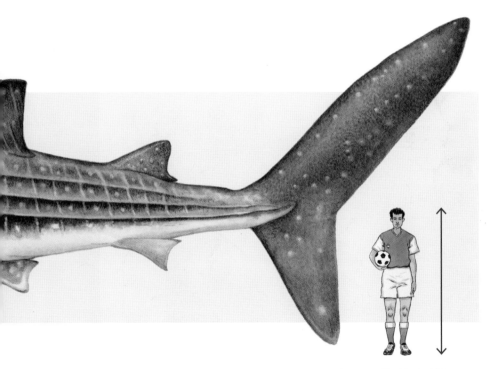

HUMAN, 6 FEET (1.8 M)

WHAT A MOUTH!

Whale sharks have huge mouths. They can be 5 feet (1.5 m) wide!

HOW DO YOU EAT?

Whale sharks have **filters** in their mouths. The whale shark sucks water into its mouth. Tiny animals and plants get caught in the filters. Then the shark swallows them.

WHALE OR SHARK?

Whale sharks are sharks, not whales! They are a type of fish. They have **gills**, are **cold-blooded**, and move their tails side-to-side.

CAN I SWIM WITH YOU?

Whale sharks don't eat people.
But whale sharks are very big and
strong. So divers should be careful
around them.

COOL PATTERN!

Whale sharks have gray backs. Their stomachs are white. They have a lot of spots. Each one's spots are different.

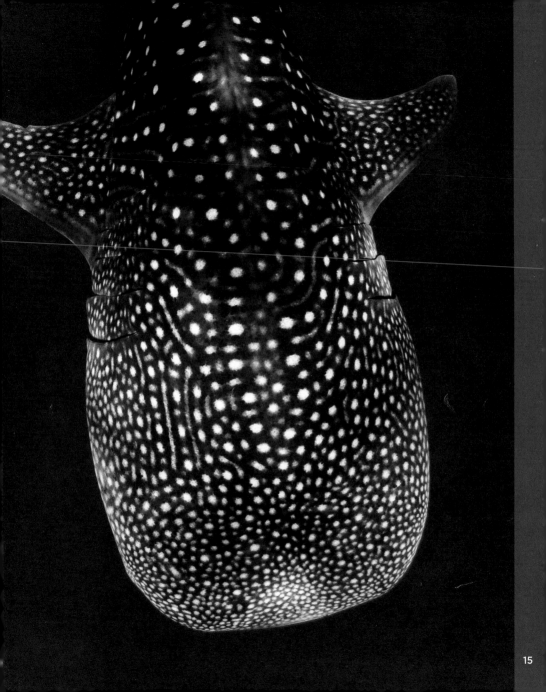

HOW OLD ARE YOU?

Whale sharks
live a long time.
They may live 100
years or longer.

WHERE DO YOU LIVE?

Whale sharks live in the ocean. They like warm water. They stay near the **equator**.

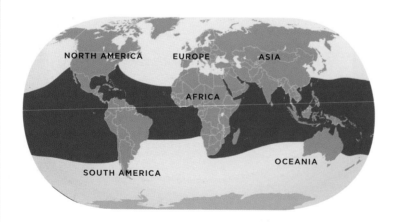

NORTH AMERICA   EUROPE   ASIA

AFRICA

SOUTH AMERICA

OCEANIA

DO YOU HAVE A FAMILY?

Whale sharks produce eggs. The eggs stay inside the mother. The babies **hatch** there. Then they are born.

QUICK QUIZ

Check your answers below!

1. Whale sharks have huge mouths. TRUE OR FALSE?

2. Whale sharks are whales. TRUE OR FALSE?

3. Whale sharks eat people. TRUE OR FALSE?

4. Whale sharks like warm water. TRUE OR FALSE?

1) True 2) False 3) False 4) True

GLOSSARY

cold-blooded – having a body temperature that changes according to the temperature of the surroundings.

equator – an imaginary line around the earth that is an equal distance from the north and south poles.

filter – a device that separates floating matter from the liquid that passes through it.

gill – an organ on a fish's side that it breathes through.

hatch – to break out of an egg.